Transcendence

Riley-Fynn Morrell

BookLeaf Publishing

Presentation by *BookLeaf Publishing*

Web: www.bookleafpub.com

E-mail: info@bookleafpub.com

ISBN: 9789357445184

First edition 2022

DEDICATION

To Megan Mumby, my poetry partner in crime

PREFACE

I have always felt a connection to the natural world, especially to the sea. It was the one thing that kept me grounded over years of fluctuation and confusion around my own sense of identity. I wanted this collection to exhibit a sense of hope, and highlight the joyful aspects of transition and self-discovery; as an LGBT+ disabled neurodivergent person, so much of the narrative around our lives can be steeped in negativity and fear. I wanted to provide an element of escape, of magic, and of positivity. We are all beautiful, and deserve to celebrate every aspect of who we are.

A couple of notes before you start:

These poems have been written over a number of years at various points in my gender exploration. As a result, some of the poems are no longer representative of how I identify, but I know they will be poignant for others, so I chose to include them in this collection. I identify as transmasculine, and enjoy using the pronouns ze/zim/zir (zee/zih-m/z-ear) alongside he/they.

One of my poems uses the term 'queer' as this is a term I use to identify myself. It is not used in a derrogatory way and is intended to be empowering.

Tattoos

I have a vision,
an image of myself
I hold in the clear pocket
of the wallet of my heart.

Hand-drawn,
exquisite watercolour shading,
line-art, colours and details
which pop against the canvas.

There are things I find
(ironic as it is)
I cannot quite articulate
with words. Things

that transform my heart
to a glowing ember, fed to my soul
and dissolved like sugar cubes,
the essence of me.

They say some wear their heart on their sleeve;
others wear the sleeve of their heart,
and there's a beauty in wanting
a piece of your soul visible,

in wanting the people you meet
watching that vision
come to life
before their eyes.

Her

Strands of hair compete with each other
to tumble in front of your sweet face –
your eyes, your smile, fighting one another
in your beauty contest. They want first place.
My hand, your cheek – like two magnets –
refuse
to disconnect. I guess the saying's true:
opposites attract. Experts could not defuse
the sparks that fly when I admire you.
admire. I should say document. I know,
by swollen and infatuated heart,
those little details crafting you. You glow.
I smile permanently. Our life can start.

So now, I ask you, what controversy?
Why should we be any less happy?

Potted

Potted plants make for nice gifts. Contained,
they grow
under restriction, existing in their purity merely
for man as green
ornaments; for observing. But they, too, observe.
They climb,
Mother Nature's periscope, defiant to fragility.
For centuries, they've survived an independent
life.
Yet still, we intervene, convinced they shall be
destroyed

unless we've rammed a rod up their backs,
destroyed
the insects who rely on them to grow,
and forced them into pots. What a life.
We owned a potted plant. It was without
flowers; a mass of green
tumbling over terracotta, possessing such a
fragility
it could have been made of ice. It could not
climb;

forced, instead, to bow to us, and allow us to
climb

in authority, submission giving us power. Its
ugliness destroyed
our perception of worth – as if the fragility
of aesthetics was worth more than a plant's
ability to grow.
No. This explosion of decaying green
deserved to fight for its independent life.

When it was clearly nearing the end of its life,
a crack appeared. Singular, at first. But as we
ignored its climb,
its fingers spread – slashes of green
blood across the terracotta. This green dragon
destroyed
its captor. We were forced to watch it grow,
fists of leaves previously hidden by the pot.
Fragility

is not often associated with the brave. But
fragility,
equally, should not be considered a hindrance in
life.
For our potted plant continued to grow
until it was no longer potted, and therefore no
longer ours. We watched it climb
horizontally. It destroyed, but it was not
destroyed.
Everything it touched turned green

with jealousy. For these once ugly, once
decaying green
tendrils made themselves beautiful. Its fragility
became its admired attribute. Our perception
was destroyed
once again; for it was alive with life,
and there is no more attractive aesthetic. The
plant will climb
no more. But it will never cease to grow.

Grow
in the eyes of the destroyer and the destroyed
alike, who will climb
together, casting a green shadow over what
fragility is. What a life.

Ze

This moment is long overdue
yet unexpected, even for me.

Such simplicity;
I've adorned badges with swears
and portraits of naked men
but this is the one
which electrifies my nerves,
makes the hairs on my arms bristle,
ready for a fight.

I change the placement three times
before stepping out of the house.
Noticeable, but
not too in-your-face.
Avoiding eye contact with everyone I pass,
heart pounding so hard against my chest
it was as if it wanted to break free.
I don't realise how fast I'm walking
until I'm forced to stop
and breathe.

Breathing quickens
as I see them in the distance.
Every possibility running through my head;

will they be shocked? Make fun?
Will they even notice it?
A part of me seems to leave me
as we start to engage in small talk.
I know I'm contributing,
but I can't hear the conversation
over the pounding in my head:
have they seen it yet
have they seen it yet
have they seen it yet
have they -

they've seen it.
they smile.
we pick up the conversation again.
somewhere, in the distance,
I hear one of them refer to me:

"ze said we should go to to the place opposite
the bank.
ze said it's zis favourite!"

and suddenly
I came back into myself.
And for the first time
I could remember,
every part of me
fitted perfectly.

The Dream

It's five thirty; you're lying in bed.
My thoughts aren't dirty. I'm watching your head
rest peacefully on a pillow that we're meant to share,
completely unaware of the lack of space you've left there
for me. Your dreams are being fed
by slow and even breaths,
and I try to lie next to you
but you're a weight of lead,
and so instead,
I thread my fingers through your hair
with such delicate care
and I stare.

I've seen your face so many times before;
if your face were a test, I know I would score
one hundred percent. I memorised the curves
of your cheeks and the curls of your eyes and my nerves
become so electric at the thought of your gaze
they could provide energy to all fifty states.
I want them to open, for your eyes to see mine,

love to break-out on your face and our lips
intertwine,
but I avert my focus to my other senses
heightened –
sense of smell, and of touch – and decide to
ignite them.
The heat of your skin
and it's smooth, moreish touch –
well, the desire to caress it
has become far too much.
The top that I'm wearing is a favourite or yours;
it adorns
so much meaning, nostalgia and allure.
Your scent clings to it like a koala bear,
its grip so tight
and this love so rare.
This top is a sponge, saturated
with time we've shared,
of the memories carved
and the looks of care
exchanged between our un-retouched eyes,
having their own affairs
as they stare
into the places even we can't reach
and ensnare
both our hearts and twist them together
until they're
unrecognisable when they're apart.
'Cos we wear

our own flags around our shoulders like capes,
but instead of coloured lines it's the other one's
face.
So beware
to all who want to cross our borders
because together
we are scared
of nothing.

So I order
myself to be patient and smile
when I see you asleep.
It could be a while,
but the truth is my happiness comes from the
fact
that just looking at your features keeps my smile
intact.
I can't help but react
to your touch and your feel.
can't pretend or act,
I cannot conceal
this crazy, unbearable, movie-like love
that so many people sing about and talk of
in poems like this. It's ridiculous, right?
But I feel that for you! Especially tonight
(or this morning, I should say)
as you lay
unmoving,
your hair unruly,

my attempts at proving
this love including soft kisses on the cheek
and barely-there whispers
to allow you to sleep.

You are a love I never thought I would have -
never thought I could have -
but when I see you resting
in your bed at five thirty
there isn't a tad
or a flicker of uncertainty
that there won't be a day when I won't want to
gaze
or be truly amazed by the fact that this love
isn't staged. It's real.
And as you lie in your bed
where I can see you and feel you
I realise that even though you may be dreaming
this is our reality. And where I was smiling
well,
now I am beaming.

Amphitrite

As I bob gently,
neck-deep in her embrace,
I ask,
"Why is it with you
I always feel so much lighter?"

She smiles, lays me back,
strokes my hair
as she replies:

"We all need to be carried sometimes."

Legal Alien

I live in a suit of glass armour
penetrable only from the outside.
Covered in mirror-film;
the 'me' you see a projection of lies
sometimes.

I made it myself – do you like it?
Fully kitted out, complete with double-glazing
over other people's minds. It even has pockets!
Perfect for storing the meltdowns, the
shutdowns,
the need to go and hide.

Nothing was provided for me
when I first came to this world. No luggage,
although now I have plenty. Rules written by
cruel ridicule and thought.
My identity hidden, so I'll never be caught.
Was it the eye contact – faked to perfection?
The obsessions diluted to acceptable
concentration?
Which part hid it best? And never made you
guess?
Because I bet you didn't. No one has. Of course,

I've not been alone. Not in concealing my status,
oh no. Misconceptions fed by misrepresentation,
misdiagnosis or misinterpretation,
coping mechanisms trending in the form of
fidget spinners
and Primark pillows covered in double-sided
sequins.

I never asked to be hidden in plain sight,
but how else would I make it through society's
borders
unquestioned? Besides, this role for so long has
been mine
there's no longer a line between my costume
and mind. Trapped

in my armour like a rodent in a zoo;
snubbed, overlooked, as if it isn't an animal too.
Vacuum-packed into glass,
always made to be smaller, neater, easier
to digest. Wouldn't want to inconvenience
anyone
with my freedom. Oh yes, how I love

to be criticised for a label assigned
that others don't think me worthy of,
then have my access denied as 'one of their
own'

until I no longer have any visible traits to
declare.
So long as they're concealed – trapped behind
glass,
locked doors and therapy sessions
and forced behind masks,

invisible, to all but me –
then I'm allowed to keep existing
in a world which was not built for me, and
refuses
to accommodate me, yet still has the audacity to
refer to me
as 'high functioning'. Well, maybe to them. But
for me,

this is the knife-edge tightrope of functioning,
and I may be a very skilled circus performer
now
but that does not mean that eventually
my feet won't start to bleed, and I vow
that the thing which still terrifies me the most
is that autism is so severely misunderstood
it wasn't until
that last line was spoken
before my status
was exposed,
my glass armour
broken.

Double-Edged Sword

"Gay sex life, unlike straight sex life, is never a private matter. When a man and a woman walk hand in hand, it is their love that they make public. When two men walk hand in hand, it is their sex life that they make public … Our words are acts; our privacy is public." – Rabbi Steven Greenberg

We walk through life,
both invisible and on display,
sometimes afforded privacy,
sometimes not,
though never being consulted
first on which
it gets to be. Our
love lives, our sex lives,
determined by whoever's hand
we're holding.
We're not unaware
of the complexities
of the human brain, and yet,
many cannot comprehend the notion

of having more than one option.
Passing privilege
melded with erasure,
passes to pride (free of judgement)
conjoined with homophobia.
The best of both worlds?
Or being forced
to slice yourself in half
in order to fit
into the two boxes provided.

Rain

Your instinct is to resist its kisses;
the ones that it leaves on the grass,
the ones it'll leave all over your clothes. You
return

to your warm and comfy bed, feeling as though
you've committed adultery. Like
you left your comfort zone, and enjoyed it.

It feels wrong to have enjoyed being in its arms
so much. You hear your lover tapping on the
window,
insistent for your return. Your hand lingers

on the wrong side
for a little too long, its kisses turning to tears
as you pull the window shut.

That's the instinct. That's the sensible thing to
do.
But I want to lie in the bed that nature has made
for me, as the rain falls,

dancing over my body like an elixir
As it covers me in an understanding

that my bed can never bring me. Clothes can be
washed,

and my bed is the comfort but the rain is the
untapped pleasure,
the energy I wasn't aware I needed,
the love of my life. Whom I yearn to give myself
fully to.

void

and we enter like a bad dream
(or rather, like a great nightmare)
and we're forced to make sense of it.
                                        of what..?
colours mixing but always making black,
dust scattered and sprinkled in the midst of
spotlessness.
the stars in our eyes as bright as the ones in the
sky,
                                    and the ones in the
sky circling black pupils,

                              making eyes,
the eyes of our universe exist in the void,
                                        in the void where
nothing exists

                  and so who is watching us?
in the void:
nothing exists   ?
regulations cease to exist.
it is our job to convey and interpret and yet
there is no beginning, there is no end
                                              and the
interpretations...

there is no beginning, there is no end. we're
forced to make our own sense of it.
because black is full of colours
and the dust mites gravitate,
never dirty but clean
on the star-scattered decorations of infinite
three-sixty wall splatters.

void means without. void means empty.
this 'empty' contains so much beauty. this
'without' holds mysteries within.
in the void:
nothing exists.
                    except the infinite possibilities,
                    except the infinite interpretations,
                    except the infinite we're taught to
understand exists there
so can something that is so full be so empty?
    can something that is so full be so empty and
if so then how would you make sense
            of this?

Part-Time Boy

It's a full-time job.
24/7 – you never know
when you might get called in.

The phone rings – 'hi there!
It's your gender dysphoria here!
You hate your chest today.
Quick – grab a top two sizes too big
and shove your hair under a beanie.
Your pronouns are he/him today,
here's your badge.
Have fun being misgendered!'

A few days pass.
You haven't heard back yet.
You go to the mirror to check,
try putting on a dress showing off your curves –
try to see yourself as 'she'
and nearly vomit into the sink
when someone who isn't you
stares back.

Is this it, then?
Is this boy still part-time
or will someone else be taking over soon?

He’s still working under the job title
printed on the birth certificate –
does that need to be updated?
What about his uniform? All this change…
it’s scary but exciting because it feels right.
It does take some people years
to find the job of their dreams,
after all.

Then,
just as he begins to settle
into a comfortable routine –
she’s back. No warning,
no call ahead of time,
no indication from management
that he might need to prepare
for yet another transition.

Mind Over Matter

It's a matter of ability.
Mind versus body -
constant battle of agility.
When my mind thinks yes
but my body screams no,
then my brain swoops low
and on the cycle goes:
Am I good enough? Am I
talking to my friends enough?
Am I working hard enough?
A capitalist slave enough?
Is the pain I'm feeling
justified or just to be expected?
Can I say I feel fatigued
without the fear of being rejected?

Mind over matter.
it's a newfound insecurity.
The things that I could do before
with ease are now obscured to me.
Even little things
are now a struggle and a chore;
going up a flight of stairs
can leave my muscles sore.
Or trying to lift a bag of shopping

could mean a day in bed,
an inability to talk,
the chronic pain chart glowing red.

I'm not asking for much:
I just want to earn a living
and for those in power to be
just slightly more forgiving.
'Mind over matter'
is a flawed and futile notion
when your mind has yet to catch up
with your finite range of motion;
when you find yourself still grieving
for the things you may not realise
are lost to you, and those memories
become things that you idolise.
We seem to think of 'young'
as a synonym for 'healthy',
and so we end up feeling
"No one's ever going to help me."
We try our best to cope alone,
take each day one by one,
yet we often end up waiting
for a 'one day' that may never come.

Does a tree ever wonder
how much longer it will stand?
Try to count each of its rings
and then create a future plan?

It's difficult to live a life
with so much damn uncertainty,
with so much fluctuation
causing flare-ups inadvertently.
I'm slowly getting used to
my own accommodations,
and accepted any ignorant bliss
will be a rare occasion,
but the ableism in this world
is simply unforgivable -
more awareness and respect
will make our lives so, so much more livable.

Mind over matter -
let's put that thinking to the side
and instead, try to find a way
for all of us to thrive.

infinite

gender is a spectrum

and spectrum implies linear
which means when most think of gender
they think

boy----------non-binary----------girl
he---------------they---------------she

and so if i am neither a boy nor a girl
i must be somewhere in the middle.
or at least, that's what i'm told.

some will see this spectrum as three options;
three tick-boxes
in which to neatly sum up and separate
the entire complexity of human experience.

others will see the middle
as a black hole of possibilities;
a place to store the nameless
or the incomprehensible,
a hoarder's nest of all we occupy
that is neither blue nor pink;

an absence of colour
altogether.

this middle holds no centre.
being made to stand there
makes many feel unbalanced.

boy----------non-binary----------girl

are we both or are we neither?

he---------------they---------------she

if blue and pink
were the two most common colours
would you see every other colour
as black?

gender is infinite

making the binary wider
will not mean we fit any neater.
we can hold that umbrella
above our heads with pride
but that does not mean underneath
we are all wearing the same flags and badges.
light through a triangle holds thousands of
colours,

many not visible
to the naked eye.

destroy the binary, the spectrum isn't linear,
etc. etc.

what does your gender look like?

stand your ground
among the infinite.

transcendence

i had only planned for it to be an escapism.
a quick break from the stresses of real life.

when i arrived, alone,
headphones singing something melancholy,
it was choppy; far too choppy to have swum in
safely. no matter; i could always sit
and watch.

the wind pressed salt to my lips
as rocks pressed awkwardly into my feet
regardless of which position i placed them.
it was cold. i liked that. i was wearing only
a t-shirt and trunks. the music fought to be heard
over the sounds of the waves crashing.

i had only planned to send one message.
a video of the sea for my friend.

one by one, i opened the apps.
stared solemnly at the pictures and posts
of an old friend. one by one,
i pressed delete. entered the name of someone
who makes me so much happier. a name
i want everyone to recognise

as much as i do.

the waves weren't letting up,
not that i expected them to. trickling
achingly closer with every surge.
i took my headphones off.
placed the phone inside my bag.

i had only planned to dip my feet in.
feel the rush of pebbles against my soles.

with the first wash of foam over my ankles,
i could feel the effort it had taken to reach me.
with every wave i took another step,
ankles joined by calves, knees, thighs,
toes burying themselves under layers of stones
to remain rooted, grounded. more and more
seaweed wrapped itself around around my legs
like vines over a tree trunk. every time
i almost lost balance, i couldn't help but giggle.

and soon, i found i couldn't stop.

i had never planned for this.
never thought i would end up here,
the sound of the waves carrying my voice
as i yelled unspoken truths wrapped in laughter
into depths, every crash a round of applause.

i embraced the inevitable,
tumbling backwards as the sea found my weak spots.
maybe there should have been pain
but i remember nothing but joy,
balled fists and open arms
stimming words so pure and raw
in a language i had never known i could speak.

i let the sea hold me
with open palms. let my body sink
below the surface hoping that,
when i finally stood up again,
the salt would have exfoliated any dead skin
that remained. knowing
that i'm allowed to want that change.
that it's a part of who i am.
that things don't always go to plan.

that maybe,
sometimes,
you don't want them to.

i don't know how long i sat there.
soaking in the seawater,
repeating those three words,
allowing them to settle peacefully
in my bones. long enough
to watch as the sky turned pink

and the dappled, white clouds
became wispy memories
dotted along the stripe of blue
in the distance.

D.I.Y

Sew and tighten
every strap, every clasp.
Fasten and fold
every fiddly scrap of fabric
to hold yourself in place. To push you up
and strap you down
in the position that's most comfortable.
Be firm. Be frugal. Forbid the futile;
don't force yourself to fit.
You've got this. You made this. You
built it all from scratch. Custom-made
to fit you perfectly
and help yourself walk taller.
Add all the design you want, extra padding
for the tough days. Write your own instructions
and
Do. It. Yourself.
Write your own instructions and
Do it for yourself.

Euphoria

The pitch of my voice -
expensive whisky
across my throat.
Using it in public
thrills me.

New hairs
adorning my legs
stand on end,
their softness beneath fingertips
a newfound comfort.

The face reflected in the mirror
has changed. Only subtly;
I can barely put my finger on it.
Textured, angular -
holding depth and detail.

The masquerade is slipping.
I can feel the excitement
fizzing, freedom
starting to escape
through my pores.

People I've known for years

are finally starting to meet me
for the first time.

And so am I.

5am

Seventeen consecutive hours spent together;
still not long enough.

Her half-drunken haze and an ink-spilled sky.
We wait for 5am to roll around because – hey,
we're up anyway, we might as well.

The exhilaration of youth and care-free decision
making.
Her rationale is butter hitting a hot pan,
convincing us that £74 on clothes and make-up
is a good idea.

Her odd socks and Star Trek pyjamas lead me to
the driver's seat.
she still carries her gin and tonic in the flask I
gave her.

We share in-jokes and selfies,
stories and memories of times we've done this
before.
Fleetwood Mac stutters a remix of Rumours
in my eighteen-year-old car CD player. We
arrive.

the window-winding handle comes off in my
hand as we drive-thru,
place our orders: hash browns and pancakes and
bacon McMuffins,
taking back extras for the flatmates.

The hash browns cannot wait;
burnt fingertips and matching tongues
accompany the drive home,
lips and steering wheel dotted with grease and
salt.
We learned, after the first trip, to always get
more than one.
I try not to get distracted by the colours of the
sun rise,
brushed-velvet clouds against skies the same
colour as her hair.

It Will Always Be Queer

After I came out
(for the first time),
I used to wish I was gay.
Tried desperately
to convince myself
that the ‘crush’ I had
on the boy in class
was merely a strong desire
for friendship. I’d overcompensate,
wearing my score of ‘5’
on the kinsey scale
like a badge of honour,
kissing my girlfriend
in the cafeteria
so that everyone
would see me and think
‘yep. Gay.’
If they didn’t question it –
maybe I would learn not to
either.

When I later came out

as trans,
that love for boys
was set free. I could admit
to myself
that the boys
I would stare at in class
were beautiful. My male gazing
came from a male gaze
so was finally allowed
to be celebrated. But

those crushes on girls
didn't go anywhere.
I still want to kiss my girlfriend.
I still want people to see.
I still want people to think
'yep. Gay.'
without question.
For them to know that,
no matter whose gaze
I'm catching,
whose hand
I'm holding,
whose lips
I'm kissing –

it will always be queer.

Refined Palette

We've always been told
we see the world in black and white.

But what they don't say
is that those are the only colours
they were willing to give us.

Pinned to stereotypes
and linear spectrums,
told we lack the capacity
to know who we are,
what we need.

The irony
and hypocrisy
of our own minds
later being deemed a product
of naive, outside influence.

When you add black to a canvas that's already
painted,
everything becomes darker. Distorted. Smudged,
until it is no longer recognisable as your own.
It's ugly. It's painful to look at. Pushed,

always, towards one or the other.
Pulled and stretched
between multiple spectrums,
twisted round them like a security blanket,
or a full body choke-hold.

Not enough for one community
and too much for another. Isolated,
yearning for more colour on your canvas,
left now to wonder
"Am I the only one?"

Boys who love boys who hate labels inside
t-shirts.
Girls who love girls who hate certain food
textures.
People of all genders believing they're
otherworldly,
with object-permeance and hyper-mobility
and a tendency to misinterpret social situations.

Thousands of us hyperfixating
on media, on transport,
on our own histories,
fiddling with necklaces, with facial hair,
with the straps of our rucksacks.
Talking 'too much'
or 'too little',

never understanding why we were told off at
school.
Who are distracted, a distraction,
who 'live in their own worlds'.

We are not the only ones.
We do not have to pick a side,
label ourselves, or limit ourselves
to just one spot on the spectrum.
Only if we want to.

We make up both communities.
We are our own community.

We each have our own canvases for a reason.
But we get to choose the colours
and what they represent
for us.

We are the artists
of our own creation.
No-one else
may take hold of our paint brushes
again.

Traffic Jam

In a moment of loss,
I look through window towards the sky
in search of a guidance, an answer, a higher
power;

I see myself instead.

Murmurations

If you visit the south coast just as sun sets
from September to March, then you might be blessed
by the wonderful sight of hundreds of starlings
all swooping and diving in unison. Never parting,
they all fly together as if joined by a string,
always moving as one; every tail, every wing.
They are common in Brighton; fly over the pier
and when I first came down here I had so much to fear.
But watching those birds would give me some hope.
Seeing that kinship; I knew I could cope.

So when dusk rolled around
sun in line with the ground: my eyes
hypnotised by those birds flying high,
working together to make patterns in the sky,
a pulse which my own heart beat alongside
I would stop, and breathe
in the salt from the sea,
watch the waves holding hands
and the starlings so free

as they mirrored each other in their stunning ballet,
every twist, turn, swoop, swirl
unrehearsed and perfect
in every way.

Time shifts in a blink. And now, looking back,
I can't help but think of my own murmuration
who love me so fiercely they feel indignation
at the notion of a predator coming my way
thus surround me with safety so I'm no longer prey.
The ones who call themselves my family
despite no blood connection or legal obligation.
The ones who support me by holding my wings
so I'll continue to fly whatever life brings.
The ones who make sure
I will soar above landscapes,
the wind on my skin, and see all the places
I now think of as home. They remind me
I'm never alone. That they're always
at the end of the phone. I'm so proud of,
together, how we've grown.

I feel so damn lucky. And I know they do too.
I can't wait for our lives. For the dreams we'll pursue.
But I yearn for those who still desperately search
for others like them. For a family they deserve.

Being lesbian, gay, bisexual or trans
has no correlation to genetics. Your ethics
may completely oppose those of all of your
relatives,
with many of us feeling we were robbed of a
heritage.
Childhoods spent trying to navigate the world
from the cis-het perspective our parents had
shown,
so when we stepped back; inspected the lack
of people like us on that family tree tapestry
we can't help but feel like we're missing that
sense
of solidarity. Of kinship. Of shared lived
experience.
And for far, far too many the situation is worse:
told their own sense of self is something
perverse.
Children and teens kicked out of their homes,
disowned by their loved ones, robbed of chances
to grow.

These actions cause damage. These tapestries
cause pain.
So we make our own flags. Start over again.
Weave the colours of the rainbow, gold thread to
embroider
our loyalty and trust and love for each other.

Pride for each others' achievements, and anger
for when any may suffer injustice or slander.
We create our own family. And that's what I
found
in this beautiful city. I'm endlessly proud.
With those flags round our shoulders or held up
to the sky,
we turn our attention to those birds flying high.
They mimick the ripples of our flags through the
air.
The threads we embroidered grow bright; the
glare
lighting up every joy on our faces.
We are loved. We are safe. We have found our
oasis.

And I know that now, when I take their hands,
wind under those flags, our capes will expand
and carry us through that crisp ocean air
and we will fly with the starlings. We will spread
that care
so it's shared among those who have yet to meet
their found families. Hold tight. There's room in
our fleet.

www.ingramcontent.com/pod-product-compliance
Lightning Source LLC
Chambersburg PA
CBHW051737130826
49812CB00033B/904
9789357445184